VALLEY COMMUNITY LIBRARY
739 RIVER STREET
PECKVILLE, PA 18452
(570) 489-1765
www.lclshome.org

Shawn Fanning

THE FOUNDER OF napster™

SHAWN FANNING

THE FOUNDER OF  napster™

UNLIMITED ACCESS
1,500,000+ SONGS

Here's what you get with your Napster Membership:
• Listen to and download an unlimited amount of music
• Enjoy 50+ commercial-free, interactive radio stations
• Discover and share music with other Napster

RENEE AMBROSEK

The Rosen Publishing Group, Inc., New York

Published in 2007 by The Rosen Publishing Group, Inc.
29 East 21st Street, New York, NY 10010

First Edition

Library of Congress Cataloging-in-Publication Data

Ambrosek, Renee.
Shawn Fanning: the founder of Napster/
Renee Ambrosek.—1st ed.
    p. cm.—(Internet career biographies)
Includes bibliographical references and index.
ISBN 1-4042-0720-1 (library binding)
1. Fanning, Shawn—Juvenile literature. 2. Napster, Inc.—
Juvenile literature. 3. Telecommunications engineers—United
States—Biography—Juvenile literature. 4. Sound—Recording
and reproducing—Digital techniques—Juvenile literature.
5. Music trade—Juvenile literature.
I. Title. II. Series.
TK5102.56.F35A43 2006
338.7'61780266092—dc22

                                        2005033558

Manufactured in the United States of America

On the cover: Foreground: Shawn Fanning. Background:
The Napster homepage today.

CONTENTS

By mid-2000, it seemed like his face was everywhere. He was an average-looking kid, usually wearing a T-shirt and grubby jeans and smiling in a shy, almost sly way. He was muscular. He always had on a baseball cap. He looked like the type of guy you'd find sitting next to you in algebra class, or like the guy down the street who owned a Camaro.

But before you knew it, you'd see his picture in another magazine. This time, he was wearing an obviously brand-new suit, with his hair cut short and very neat. Now, he looked like a kid on the fast track; a kid who understood the power of first impressions.

None of the photos seemed to match. The magazines were tossing out adjectives to describe him right and left, but they didn't seem to match, either. "Gearhead," one called him. Others said he was a "super-genius."

"A renegade."

"Average."

"A wunderkind."

"Sweet."

"Driven."

"Unassuming."

Shawn Fanning during the height of his fame in 2000. Sitting on the rooftop of his apartment building in California, Shawn is wearing one of his usual outfits of T-shirt, cargo pants, and baseball cap. However, despite the unassuming "typical kid" image that Shawn portrayed, the media at the time was accusing him of being "the most dangerous man in the music biz."

There were so many contradicting descriptions. The most amazing part of it all was that just a year before, no one had ever even heard of him. All of his notoriety had seemed to spring up overnight.

And now, across the United States, people were asking themselves, "Who in the heck is this kid, anyway?"

His name was Shawn Fanning. And according to the cover of *Rolling Stone* magazine, he was "the most dangerous man in the music biz."

CHAPTER ONE

FROM ORDINARY TO EXTRAORDINARY

There was nothing in Shawn Fanning's birth and early childhood to suggest that he was going to someday be extraordinary. In fact, his beginnings were more the stuff of cautionary tale than of legend. He was a poor kid—not exactly from "the wrong side of the tracks," but certainly not from the "right" side either—who had to live through more before high school than a lot of people have to deal with their whole lives.

Shawn's mother, Colleen Fanning, met Shawn's father at a house party in the working-class town of Rockland, Massachusetts. The party was being thrown by Colleen's family, in honor of her older brother's graduation from high school. The party was a surprising success—only a few hundred friends had been invited, but a few thousand showed up.

Colleen's fourteen-year-old brother, John, took advantage of the situation and wandered through the crowd, asking for donations. This was to be John's first big entrepreneurial experiment, and he did quite well, collecting a few thousand dollars to help pay for the party.

If anyone could have looked into the future on that night, they probably would have been impressed at the amount of foreshadowing taking place. The scene had many elements that would occur again eighteen years later: music, teenagers, unexpected crowds, and John Fanning in the center of it all, transforming a party into a business venture.

But back in Rockland, the kids couldn't see into the future. Most of them were just there to see the band that the family had hired to play at the party. The band was named MacBeth, and they played mostly Aerosmith covers mixed with some originals. They were a big hit with the crowd—and not only because of their musical skill. MacBeth had another crowd-pleaser: a good-looking, charismatic lead guitarist named Joe Rando. Sixteen-year-old Colleen Fanning was smitten with eighteen-year-old Joe, and it didn't take long for the two to become a couple. However, young love screeched to a halt several months later when Colleen told Joe that she was pregnant. The new father-to-be abruptly broke off the relationship, leaving Colleen to raise their child without him.

DIFFICULT BEGINNINGS

However, Colleen was far from alone. The Fannings were a large, blue-collar, Irish family, and Colleen had seven brothers and sisters. All eight of the Fanning kids lived together in their three-bedroom home. Baby Shawn made nine in November of 1980. Not long after Shawn was born, the family moved to nearby Brockton, Massachusetts, where Shawn spent his early childhood.

After a few difficult years as a single mother, Colleen married Raymond Verrier, an ex-marine who drove a delivery truck for a bread company. The couple had four more children, which put pressure on the already-stretched family finances. "Money was always a pretty big issue," Shawn was to say later about his childhood. "There was a lot of tension around that."[1]

The family lived near Brockton's housing projects. The neighborhood was pretty rough, which was sometimes hard on the shy, mild-mannered, young Shawn. According to his mother, Shawn dealt with his tough surroundings by withdrawing and becoming more introspective, trying to block out the stresses around him. "He went inside himself real deep and said, 'I want to get out of this.' Even though it meant losing him a little bit, it's what I wanted for him," Colleen would later recall.[2]

When Shawn was around twelve years old, his home life got even more difficult. His mom and stepdad separated. Unable to support all five of her kids alone, Colleen was forced to place Shawn and his half siblings into foster homes for several months. Shawn relied on school, sports, and music to take his mind off the situation, throwing himself wholeheartedly into everything that he tried. After all, when you don't have any free time, you don't have much time to feel sorry for yourself. He soon proved to be an excellent student, a talented and dedicated athlete, and an avid beginning guitarist.

By the time Shawn had reached high school, the family had reunited and things were looking

SHAWN MEETS HIS BIOLOGICAL FATHER

When Shawn was seventeen years old, his uncle John located Shawn's biological father on the Internet. Joe Rando and Shawn had never met, although Shawn had known about Joe's existence since he was seven. John discussed his discovery with Shawn's mom, Colleen, who agreed that there didn't seem to be any harm in contacting Joe. A meeting between Joe and Shawn was arranged. Colleen would later tell reporter Joseph Menn that she was surprised when she saw Shawn and Joe together for the first time. She couldn't get over the striking physical similarities between the two, even down to the way they walked. There were other eerie similarities as well; Joe also had a methodical, scientific mindset paired with a business edge, earning a degree in physics as well as an MBA. He had also owned some small computer software firms in the past. Shawn and Joe hit it off, and Shawn stayed in touch with him throughout the Napster craze that was to follow.

up. They were able to move to Harwich Port, a small, middle-class seaside town near Cape Cod that boasted a good public school system. Colleen encouraged Shawn in every way she could think of, hoping that his dedication and drive would help him escape his blue-collar surroundings someday. She also reached out to her younger brother John to help her motivate young Shawn, hoping that her brother's ambition would rub off on her young son. "He's like Shawn in a different way," explained Colleen. "He wanted out of the situation that he started in. It was the motivation to succeed that I wanted Shawn to pick up on."[3]

An Exceptional Student

By this time, John Fanning, who had shown such entrepreneurial promise at fourteen, was working as a businessman in the relatively new, cutting-edge field of computer programming. Although he hadn't yet broken into the computer business big-time, he was keeping his head above water with a reasonably lucrative gaming software company and was in a position to mentor young Shawn when it came to business and finance.

John was also in a position to give Shawn things that his parents weren't able to provide for him. One of John's more impressive gifts was a car—a dark purple BMW Z3—that had originally been the company car of one of John's former employees. A car like that was quite an accessory for an average kid from Harwich Port, and although Shawn wasn't the type to be snobby or put on airs, he also didn't mind the celebrity that the car provided him.

John also paid Shawn for each A on his report card, ensuring that Shawn continued to do quite well in school. Not that it was an especially difficult task for Shawn, though. Shawn was a popular, well-rounded high school student, liked by most of his classmates. He also showed an early ability to focus intensely when need be. "A lot of kids can tune out, but he was right on track. He was an A student without trying. He was a nice, generous, level-headed young man," Richard Besciak, his history teacher, would later remember.[4]

In spite of his excellent grades, Shawn's family expected that it would be his talent in sports that would provide his ticket to college. Shawn played several school sports, including tennis and basketball, and had developed into what coaches like to call "an exceptional team player." Team sports taught Shawn many of the lessons that would serve him well later in life, such as how to take criticism and how to work well with others. One friend of Shawn's would later notice about him:

> Shawn is able to concentrate, and collaborate and appropriate if necessary.

He's also able to handle criticism. Most alpha-geeks can't take criticism. They'll get into arguments. Shawn actually listens and takes the best part of what you say.[5]

Of all the sports that Shawn excelled at, though, it was his exceptional talent in baseball (one year he batted over .650) that seemed to be his best shot at a ticket out of Harwich Port. Shawn's family was counting on a baseball scholarship to provide Shawn with a college education, and it seemed very likely that he would be offered one.

A TWIST OF FATE

In 1996, when he was a sophomore in high school, Shawn received a gift from his uncle John that changed everything—an Apple Macintosh 512+ computer. John thought that the computer would simply give Shawn another outlet to explore—another hobby to add to the long list of things that he was interested in. However, Shawn surprised everyone with the immediate intensity of his interest in computers. "I saw this as a way for him to work his way out of his situation . . . [but] he absorbed the stuff faster than anyone I've ever known," John recalls.[6]

The Apple Macintosh 512+ computer (shown above) was an early-generation Apple computer. It was manufactured in the early to mid-1980s, and was probably nearly ten years old when Shawn's uncle, John Fanning, gave it to him as a gift. Despite the age of the computer, Shawn was able to learn programming very quickly on the Mac.

From the beginning, Shawn spent a considerable amount of time on his computer, doing homework and chatting on the Internet, all the time with the radio blaring at full volume in the background. In fact, he was so taken with his new present from his uncle John that he quickly gave up sports and many of his other hobbies to devote himself to learning about computers full-time. One of Shawn's high school classmates remembers his obsession, saying:

> [Computers] really seemed to consume
> him. There were those who were doing
> it just as a hobby, for games, or to
> cheat in school. Shawn went through
> that phase, but it was just a starting
> point. He was quickly beyond that,
> doing much more sophisticated things.[7]

Shawn learned so quickly, in fact, that John soon offered him an internship at Chess.net during his summer breaks from school. Chess.net was John's current software gaming company, based in the nearby port city of Hull. Shawn spent all of his free time at the company office, learning programming as quickly as he could from the

Chess.net staff, most of whom were students or recent graduates from Carnegie-Mellon University's renowned computer science program. Those early days learning at Chess.net were special for Shawn, as he would recollect later:

> I was just getting into programming, so I spent a lot of my time just fiddling with projects and hanging out. I have a really fond memory of that time, but I think I could have taken better advantage of it in terms of learning. Eventually, I transitioned into doing some programming for the Web back end. I built the Web store [for the company]. I was doing a lot of network programming and Unix programming and stuff. I was around computer guys, so it gave me a chance to learn.[8]

However, Chess.net wasn't the only place where Shawn was learning about programming. At around this same time, Shawn also discovered Internet Relay Chat (IRC). IRC is a huge text-messaging forum for computer enthusiasts around the world. It has several different channels (or "rooms") covering almost every computer topic that you could imagine.

w00w00

Shawn quickly became a fixture on IRC, making friends with other computer enthusiasts, most of whom were also young fledgling programmers. They discussed programming, code, and software, coming up with new ideas together and helping each other with difficult programming problems.

As Shawn made a name for himself on IRC, he was invited to join "w00w00," a private IRC channel whose members were more sophisticated and talented computer hackers. Membership into w00w00 was by invitation only, and to be invited, you had to prove yourself to be more than just a wanna-be. Shawn was not only learning, but he was learning fast enough to be noticed by the IRC elite.

Most everyone on w00w00 was known only by a screen name; this was to keep a sense of anonymity when discussing hacking issues. Shawn chose his screen name based on his nickname back at high school, where his friends would often good-naturedly rag him about his usually matted, unruly, curly hair. He called himself Napster.

By the time Shawn was ready to consider college choices, he was already pretty sure about where he wanted to go and what he wanted to study. The only school he was serious about was Carnegie-Mellon University in Pittsburgh, Pennsylvania. He wanted to major in computer science there, as so many of his friends and

Shillman Hall on the campus of Northeastern University in Boston, Massachusetts. Although Shawn had his heart set on attending Carnegie-Mellon University, he ended up enrolling in Northeastern instead; it was his only "fallback" school.

coworkers at his uncle's company had done. His grades were good, his extracurriculars were good, and his programming knowledge was excellent, but even that was not enough. Carnegie-Mellon was very competitive, and Shawn didn't make it in.

Shawn had applied to only one fallback school—Northeastern University in nearby Boston. According to Shawn's uncle John, Shawn applied to only two schools because he couldn't afford to pay the forty-dollar application fee for more than two, and he was too proud to ask John for the money to apply to anywhere else. Whether or not this was the case, two applications were enough. Northeastern not only accepted Shawn but placed him in junior- and senior-level computing courses as an entering freshman.

A SIMPLE QUESTION

Even so, Shawn was bored at Northeastern. He spent his first semester partying, hanging out in the dorm with his roommates, and driving back to his uncle's office every time his schedule would allow. He was a lot happier and more comfortable with the computer programmers who were already out of school and working—already

THE MANY HATS OF HACKERS

In the computer world, the term "hacker" doesn't necessarily refer to someone who is breaking the law with a computer. In general, a hacker is just a programmer with exceptional skill. While there are outlaw hackers ("black hats," or "crackers") who spend their time trying to break into systems and do damage to computer programs, there are also good hackers ("white hats") who are simply interested in complicated coding and figuring out how to make existing programs stronger by identifying their weaknesses. In fact, many white-hat hackers get hired by computer firms to help them find software problems and improve their overall security.

The w00w00 computer channel on IRC was home to both white hats and black hats, with hackers from both sides exchanging tips and information. Shawn would later identify himself as having been a white hat, admitting that early on, one of his main interests in computers was in understanding security issues. However, because IRC had a cross section of different types of hackers, the programmers who would go on to help Shawn write the Napster program were a mix of both white and black hats.

doing something important and writing programs to be used, rather than writing programs for a grade. It seemed to Shawn that school was just holding him back and wasting his time.

However, it was at school, during his first semester, that an offhand comment from one of Shawn's roommates got him to thinking. It was just a simple complaint, made out of frustration by a roommate whose name Shawn wouldn't even be able to remember later. Shawn and his roommates had been discussing Internet music files, a recent innovation on the computer scene, when Shawn's roommate complained about the fact that the music files were too difficult to find on the Internet.

The more Shawn thought about the complaint, the more it bothered him. His roommate was right. Music files were hard to find. But they didn't need to be. It seemed to Shawn that there should be a much easier way for him and his friends to find the music that they wanted on the Internet. Why wasn't there?

Because of that simple question, Shawn's life was to change forever, going almost overnight from ordinary to extraordinary.

CHAPTER TWO

BRINGING UP NAPSTER

When Shawn was a college freshman in 1998, there weren't many people who listened to music on their computers. For the most part, only college kids and hard-core music buffs even tried. Although store-bought CDs would play on computer systems with CD drives, most people didn't store music files of any type on their computer hard drives.

This was not because the technology wasn't available. MP3 files had been invented as early

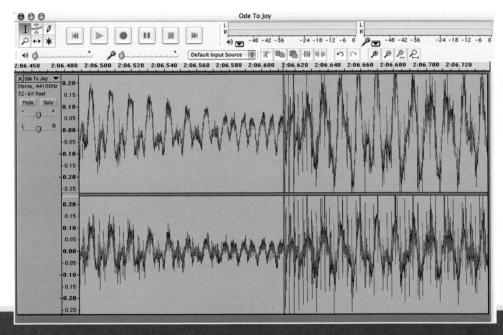

A music track is shown being played through an MP3 editor program. Common use of the MP3 file technology paved the way for the success of Napster by making it possible to download song files much more quickly than before.

as 1995, and they proved to be an excellent way to store music files, as well as to send the files over the Internet. Before MP3 technology, standard music files were so large that they would eat up hard-drive space. They were slow to download, too. It would take up to two hours to download a song on a 56K Internet connection (the traditional dial-up connection that most people used at that time, at 56 kilobits per second). However, converted to an MP3 file, the same song would take only about twelve minutes to download on a 56K connection. Using a high-speed Internet connection, the download time would be cut down even more.

So if the MP3 technology was out there and it was good, why didn't more people use MP3s? The problem was in finding the MP3 files in the first place. Most MP3 files floating around on the Internet were a result of someone who had ripping software—such as Winamp—that allowed them to convert a CD audio track into an MP3. These MP3s were usually stored on people's personal Web sites, and to find them, people had to use a search engine such as MP3.com or Scour.net.

However, the search engines available at the time for MP3s weren't very user-friendly. More often than not, they brought back results that included out-of-date Web sites or broken links. The few MP3 files that could be readily found were usually files from unknown, undiscovered bands that kept their files up to date hoping that they would gain a wider audience if people found them on the Internet.

MP3s SIMPLIFIED

MP3 is the shortened name for Motion Picture Expert Group Audio Layer III—quite a long name for something designed to make things more simple! It's an audio compression format that was developed by Fraunhofer Gesellschaft, a German company. Basically, it's an algorithm that allows a user to take large music files and reformat them in a way that turns them into much, much smaller files (MP3 files), while still preserving the quality of the music. The process of converting a large sound file (like one found on a store-bought CD) to an MP3 is referred to as ripping.

The technology works because MP3 is "perceptual." This means that it only deals with music sounds that can be perceived, or recognized, by the human ear. Traditional sound files record all waves of sound, even those sound waves that are too high or too low for human ears to detect. It takes up a lot of memory to save all of those waves digitally. MP3 evaluates the music and shaves off all of the sounds that humans wouldn't be able to hear anyway. Then it finds sound waves that are similar in tone and compresses them together. This means that there is some loss of quality in an MP3 file, but not enough that most humans can detect the difference. However, the difference in file size is huge. With MP3 files, users can download music at a fraction of the time that they could with older, large audio formats.

A Sense of Community

Unfortunately, it was much harder to find MP3s of music from more established bands that had already been signed by record companies. People who posted MP3s of popular groups tended to change their Web sites regularly to make them harder to find. Legally, these types of MP3s were suspect. Although the courts had decided that ripping music was legal for personal use, sharing those ripped songs with others was more of a gray area. This meant that most MP3s in existence were never posted on the Internet. They just stayed on the hard drives of the people who'd ripped them. Those people who did want to share had to be careful. Web sites that contained MP3s of popular bands moved around quite a bit. This made finding them using the old, slow search engines nearly impossible.

This didn't seem right to Shawn. Like most other college students, he enjoyed sitting around and discussing his favorite music with his friends. He liked meeting other people who loved the same bands as he did. He appreciated the sense of community that music fans shared. It was like the sense of community that he found on the IRC and that he shared with people interested in his other passion, programming. Why couldn't he find that same sense of community on the Internet when it came to music?

Shawn began to think about how cool it would be to go to a Web site, find files of his favorite bands, and chat with other fans all at the same time. He wasn't thinking about founding a business, or whether or not there would be legal problems with his idea. He wasn't even thinking about becoming rich or famous because of his idea. He was just thinking about how great it would be to easily find, talk to, and share music with other people who were interested in the same bands that he liked. A Napster spokesman would later sum up this entire idea in an interview, saying:

> People are naturally passionate about music, naturally want to share it; artists naturally want to create and share their music and find their fans: That's what music is all about. Now we have the Internet—why can't we do some of that there?[1]

Once Shawn had the initial idea, he started to think of ways to make it happen. He knew enough about programming to know that there was probably a way to create a program that could do exactly what he wanted. At first, he just toyed with the idea some in his free time. However, as he began to realize that the technology was definitely out there, he became much more focused. He was as focused as only a hard-core hacker gets when working on a computer problem.

A LITTLE HELP FROM SOME FRIENDS

Shawn wanted to build a program that would put together all of the best parts of programs that were already in existence. It would be able to instant message like IRC did, so that fans could talk to one another in real time. It would be able to search and filter like the very best search engines available. And it would be able to share files like Microsoft Windows did.

This last part presented an early problem for Shawn. He didn't know anything about Windows programming. As a hard-core hacker, Shawn had been taught computer programming using Unix, a much more advanced operating system. However, in order for his idea to work, it would have to be useable by the average person— and the average person was running a Windows operating system.

Shawn realized that he needed to teach himself how to program with the Windows operating system, so he ordered a book about Windows programming on Amazon.com. After he got the book, he studied it like most people cram for exams—which was just as well, because since he had started thinking seriously about his program, he hadn't really been paying attention to any of his college exams anymore. Shawn once again proved to be a quick learner, though, because in a few short weeks he had mastered Windows well enough to write code for it.

But Windows was not Shawn's only hurdle to jump—there were other problems that he couldn't immediately work out. This is where his friendships with his fellow hackers on w00w00 became invaluable. When Shawn hit a barrier that he couldn't find a way around, he would post his problem on w00w00. "I could always ask them a question about protocol design or just shoot a question to the channel and have somebody answer it," Shawn would later explain. "I wouldn't have been able to write Napster without IRC and these groups of people. The amount of time it would have taken me to find the answers in books or find the resources I needed, I would never have finished it on time. I definitely owe a lot of people."[2]

IRC group feedback wasn't always positive, though. When Shawn explained that he was working on a program that would enable users to share music files with one another, he was surprised that some hackers were very pessimistic about it. Some of them thought that the program sounded too complicated. Some were just negative in general. "It's a selfish world, and nobody wants to share," he was told by an older hacker.[3]

DRIVE

Instead of discouraging him, this sort of response just pushed Shawn to work harder. He was determined to prove that his idea was a good one and that his program would run. A friend of Shawn's explained it later in an interview, saying:

> Shawn Fanning is an extremely determined character, young as he is. Part of the spirit behind Napster, in my opinion, was Shawn Fanning thinking this was a good idea, and other people telling him it wouldn't work, simple as that. I believe he was driven more by

the desire to prove to everyone that he was right than he was by any realization or recognition of a potential revolution.[4]

Shawn was also driven by the fear that someone else would create the program before he could. Once he started working on the project, it started to seem to him that the solution to his problem of finding music on the Internet was simple. He became worried that maybe it was so simple that other people would finish a version of the program before he did.

Soon Shawn would find himself so obsessed with finishing his program that he found it hard to focus on other things—like college. Toward the end of his first semester he started to spend longer amounts of time in Hull. The weekends that he would spend at his uncle's office would get extended, as it became more and more difficult to pull himself away from his program and get back to campus. Finally, he managed to survive his first freshman semester and was thrilled to be able to spend his entire winter break at his uncle's office, working on the program.

The intensity of his focus impressed the other programmers at Chess.net. "When he gets interested in something new, he dedicates all of his resources to mastering it, and then he goes beyond that. He just has a single-mindedness that made him proficient," remembers one Chess.net employee.[5] Added another, "I don't think people can appreciate how hard he worked. This was his way out of the 'hood, out of everything."[6]

It was Shawn Fanning's passion for music and desire to reach out to other music fans that inspired the creation of Napster. In this photograph taken on May 25, 2000, his love of music is evident. Shawn plucks his Les Paul guitar near a stack of CDs during a break from programming.

Shawn was coding for hours at a time at his uncle's office, concentrating on each little piece of the program for as long as it took him to finish that piece. He kept himself awake for as long as he could, sometimes working up to sixty hours straight, surviving only on delivery pizza and Red Bull energy drinks. As he got farther and farther into his program, he began to realize that he was really on to something. It was something big.

But by January 1999, Shawn's winter break was over. He reluctantly accepted a ride back to school from his cousin Brian. He didn't want to go back. He wasn't sure how he was going to finish his program and go to school at the same time. At that moment, his program was much more important to him than his Northeastern classes were. The classes had always seemed boring and too easy to begin with.

When they arrived at the school, Shawn got out of Brian's car and walked up to his dorm. When he reached the door of the building, he stopped for a moment. Then he turned around and slowly walked back to his cousin's car. He got into the car and told his cousin to drive him back to Hull. Just like that, Shawn Fanning had decided to quit school. His cousin told him that he was crazy, and Shawn himself admitted that he might be. Shawn was torn by his decision. But as he explained it later, he felt that if he stayed in college he wouldn't be able to devote himself fully to either his program or his schoolwork:

> [In college] I was going to do 50 percent of two things, and I wouldn't have ever been satisfied. So I just decided to go for it and left everything at the school and didn't talk to any of my roommates. Because if I had talked to them, they would have said, "What are you doing, you're crazy," and convinced me to come back or make me feel bad about it. So I basically disappeared for a few months. And then finally once I had launched [my program], and they saw what I was doing, they felt a little better about it. I think they could tell I was never happy—well, not not happy about school, but I never felt like I was supposed to be there.[7]

Shawn's mother, predictably, was a lot less understanding about his decision—at least in the beginning. When Shawn told her the news, she broke down in tears. Shawn would have been

THE IRC's UNSUNG HEROES

As Shawn was working on his program, he relied a lot on the knowledge and advice of his friends on the IRC network. Two of them, Jordan Ritter and Sean Parker, would go on to play huge roles in the foundation of Napster as a business—such huge roles, in fact, that Shawn credits them as being cofounders of Napster. Other friends from w00w00 were also instrumental in fleshing out the details of intricate areas of programming. One

Napster cofounder Jordan Ritter, pictured here, was the architect behind the server software that supported the millions of Napster users.

of the first hackers who saw the Napster program was Seth McGann, who was enthusiastic and encouraging about Shawn's idea from the beginning. Another user, Dug Song, was able to tell Shawn where to look for more information to help him solve specific problems that he was encountering. The w00w00 member Evan Brewer was one of the first people responsible for running the central server for Napster. The w00w00 group also had the distinction of being the first group to test the program, as Shawn sent out early Napster trials on w00w00 and asked for comments and advice.

the first in his immediate family to graduate from college, and in Colleen Fanning's eyes, he was giving up his only ticket to success. "It was tough," Colleen said later. "I had built this thing up about him going to college. He knew how disappointed I was."[8] However, when she saw how serious Shawn was about his decision, she backed down some and admitted that he should trust his instincts.

Shawn's uncle John was a lot less disturbed by Shawn's decision. As a businessman, he was beginning to think that Shawn's idea might end up having some commercial potential. To John, this looked like a possible moneymaking opportunity. He encouraged Shawn and began to seriously look into how to go about incorporating Shawn's idea into a company.

As for Shawn, he spent the next few months doing what he loved, solely because he loved doing it. He worked around the clock with his laptop, pizza, and Red Bull. Time flew by, but he was oblivious to it. In a few months, Shawn finally emerged from his self-imposed exile. On his computer was a brand-new program, one that did everything that he had hoped it would. He called the program Napster.

CHAPTER THREE

How a Pop Culture Icon Was Created

When Shawn finally finished his program, he had a lot to be proud of. Napster was brilliant. It solved all of the problems that people had encountered while looking for MP3 files with one bold stroke—it simply eliminated the middleman.

In the earliest days of the Internet, all of the information on the World Wide Web was connected using a computer-to-computer system. All of the computers communicated directly with one another and shared information between each other. However, as the number of computer users grew and the amount of information to be stored grew, the Internet moved to a server system.

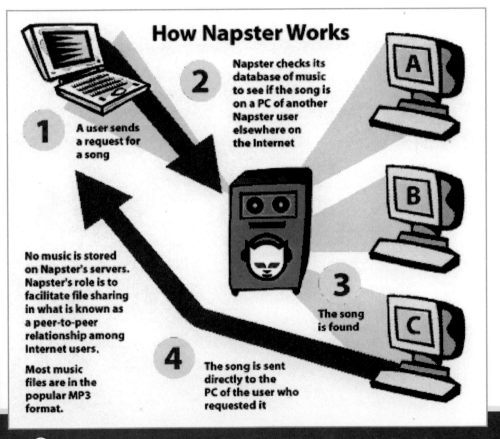

How Napster Works

2 Napster checks its database of music to see if the song is on a PC of another Napster user elsewhere on the Internet

1 A user sends a request for a song

No music is stored on Napster's servers. Napster's role is to facilitate file sharing in what is known as a peer-to-peer relationship among Internet users.

Most music files are in the popular MP3 format.

3 The song is found

4 The song is sent directly to the PC of the user who requested it

Instead of a user searching for a song using "robots," (which would often find dead or broken links), the Napster program was able to do a direct search of the hard drives of other users and find live links, sending the live links almost immediately back to the user.

This meant that information was stored in huge databases on servers all over the world, like enormous computer libraries of information. As this became the norm, it meant that computers weren't really communicating directly with one another anymore. Instead, when a computer user tried to find a piece of information (for example, an MP3 file) using a search engine, the engine

Filename	Filesize	Bitrate	Freq	Length	User	Connection	Ping
incomplete_other_artist\Tito Puentes Golden Latin Jazz Allstars - Oye Como ...	3,696,640	128	44100	3:51	bdenzler	DSL	343
incomplete_other_artist\[Marty Robbins] The Fastest Gun Around.mp3	542,304	128	44100	0:39	bdenzler	DSL	343
incomplete_other_artist\Ravi Shankar - Chants Of India 04 - Asato Maa.mp3	2,449,408	128	44100	2:35	bdenzler	DSL	343
other artist\Engelbert Humperdinck - White Christmas.mp3	9,277,648	320	44100	3:52	bdenzler	DSL	343
other artist\Grateful Dead - Franklin's Tower - Reggae Style.mp3	4,635,458	128	44100	4:48	bdenzler	DSL	343
Unknown Artist - You seriously have to listen to this.mp3	462,848	318	16000	0:17	sam113...	Cable	383
MP3z\artist - The Way Life Is' By Drag-On featuring Case.mp3	4,726,784	128	44100	4:54	burg651	Cable	386
MP3z\artist - Opposite Of H20' By Drag-On featuring Jadakiss.mp3	3,540,992	128	44100	3:41	burg651	Cable	386
Various Artist - Perfect Day 97.mp3	3,722,344	128	44100	3:53	falkstad	ISDN-128K	398
Liszt\Liszt - Etude 'Un sospiro' - Czilfra-artist.mp3	2,752,512	128	44100	2:53	lskjdflkjl...	Unknown	504
Music\Waiting To Exhale - Original Soundtrack Album - Various Artist - Count...	3,199,083	96	44100	4:26	Jzfork9	56K	511
Track 03_artist.mp3	4,054,332	128	44100	4:13	immusic	Cable	514
Track 02_artist.mp3	6,228,974	128	44100	6:26	immusic	Cable	514
Track 01_artist.mp3	4,731,456	128	44100	4:54	immusic	Cable	514
Track 04_artist.mp3	4,514,505	128	44100	4:41	immusic...	Cable	514
Track 05_artist.mp3	4,105,323	128	44100	4:16	immusic...	Cable	514
mixer in track 01_Artist_0721011750.mp3	180,686	128	44100	0:17	immusic...	Cable	514
Album\Reflex - Keep In Touch-Artist.mp3	7,041,024	160	44100	5:49	rotimco	56K	527

Returned 100 results.

Get Selected Songs | Add Selected User to Hot List

Online (keyscreen): Sharing 491 files. | Currently 740,043 files (2,991 gigabytes) available in 5,873 libraries.

One of the best things about Napster was how easy it was to use. A user could look for a song using either the artist name or song title, and then he or she would get a list of all of the available files that matched, as well as several vital details about the matching files.

would send out "robots" to examine the database indexes of all of the servers it could find, trying to find files on those indexes that matched the user's request.

However, the robots could only report whether or not the files a user wanted were supposed to be on a server, based on what the server's indexes said. Unfortunately, though, they couldn't confirm if the files were actually there or not. This meant that once the user tried to link to the file, there was a good chance that the information would no longer be available. This is similar to a librarian searching the library's card catalog and telling you that the book you're asking for is supposed to be in the library, but not looking on the shelves to tell you whether or not it's actually there.

P2P

In essence, Napster just eliminated the middleman—the server. It did this using something called peer-to-peer technology, or P2P for short. P2P is a way of making computers operate more like they did in the days before servers. It enables computers to send information directly to one another instead of making them go to a server to get information files.

P2P technology wasn't invented by Shawn. In fact, a few other programs on the Internet were already using it. However, the programs using P2P were mostly specialized applications, nothing that the average computer user would normally have any contact with. (The only exception to this was Usenet newsgroups, which used P2P technology.) Napster was the first program to really bring P2P to the attention of the general public.

But despite the fact that Napster was the most well-known P2P program in the world during its heyday, it didn't use P2P exclusively. Napster also used central servers. However, unlike most servers, the Napster central servers never held any of the information files themselves. Instead, the Napster central servers only held indexes of files, telling computers where to go to get the files they were looking for.

As one observer pointed out, it was similar to an old telephone switchboard: "Like a telephone switchboard operator in the old days, the Napster system would take an inquiry for a specific song from someone, find another person who had a matching offering, connect the two, and then hang up and let them finish their transaction in private."[1]

HOW IT WORKS

Here's how Napster worked. As a new Napster user, first you would download the Napster program onto your computer's hard drive. Then you'd direct the Napster program to the location of your MP3 files on your hard drive. The Napster program would take over from there.

When you opened Napster on your computer, you would see an interface screen where you could type in the name of the song that you were looking for. The Napster program would connect to the Napster central server and search the server index to see what other Napster user had a copy of that song on his or her hard drive. Then the central server would connect your computer to the other Napster user's computer so that you could download the MP3 directly off of the other user's hard drive.

While all of this was happening, your Napster program would report a list of all of the songs that you had on your hard drive back to the Napster central server. This meant that any other user could be connecting to your hard drive and copying something off of it at the same time that you were copying something from someone else. In short, this would turn your

NAPSTER VS. GNUTELLA

While Napster was explained in most news reports as being a peer-to-peer program, it wasn't purely P2P. Napster did need to use central servers to hold the indexes of all of the files available on user hard drives. This is known as a centralized P2P system,

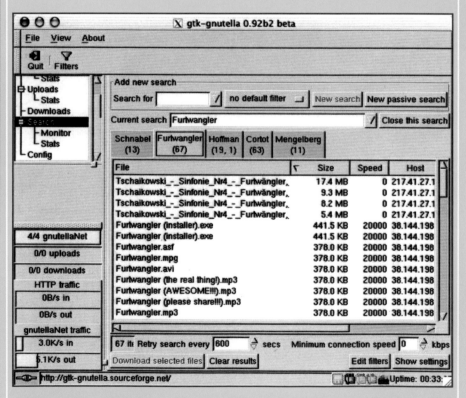

This is the user interface of the Gnutella program, Napster's first big competitor. Although Gnutella had the advantage of being "untraceable," the user interface was more complicated to use than the Napster interface, and the program's search time was slower.

and it has some disadvantages. One of the most obvious is that there is a traceable record on the central server showing just what is being offered for download at any given time.

Less than a year after Napster was first released, the first serious Napster copycat showed up on the scene. Created by Justin Frankel, another teenage hacker (and a friend of Shawn's), Gnutella was released on March 14, 2000. Gnutella was different from Napster in one very important way: it was a decentralized P2P program. Instead of using central servers, Gnutella sent out a search for material that operated in a pattern that looked something like a family tree. A request for a song would be sent to one central hub, which would pass it on to more hubs, each of which would pass it on to even more hubs, and so on, with the search ever expanding.

The problem with the decentralized system was that with each pass between hubs, the system slowed down. This meant that the more users that were on the system, the slower the program worked. However, in the long run, the absence of a central server also meant that Gnutella searches couldn't ever be traced to any one person or server, making it virtually lawsuit-proof.

computer into a miniserver, letting other Napster users connect directly to your hard drive to download information. When you logged onto Napster, your song files would be added to the Napster central server list. When you logged off, they would be removed.

This meant that for the first time in the history of MP3 sharing, Napster users were able to see, moment to moment, every single user in the system that had a copy of the file that they were looking for. There were no missing files or empty links; if the song was there, users knew it immediately. But this was just the tip of the iceberg. Shawn's program went beyond just solving the problem of missing files and empty links. Shawn

A student at New York University uses Napster in 2001. College students were the first users of Napster, and they passed the program across the country with amazing speed, creating a huge "community of music lovers," just as Shawn had envisioned.

was also hoping to create a sense of community. In order to accomplish this, Napster had some really cool built-in features.

CUSTOM FEATURES

Napster not only let users search by song name, but by artist name, too. They could find rare tracks by their favorite bands that they might not have even known existed. There were chat rooms that fans could go into to talk, as well as an instant messaging feature that allowed people to start immediate conversations with the people that they were copying files from. A feature called "hot lists" enabled users to look for other people who had downloaded music from their favorite artists, and then get recommendations from those people about similar bands that they might not have ever heard about. Napster fostered a community in every possible way that Shawn dreamed that it would.

The best part of the Napster program was that it had an extremely user-friendly interface. It was simple to use—even for people who didn't have a lot of computer knowledge. This simplicity wasn't entirely intentional, though. It was a result of the incredible speed at which Shawn wrote the program. Shawn was in a hurry to finish his program and get it to the public. He just didn't have the time to make it any more complicated. "I had to focus on functionality, to keep it real simple," Shawn said. "With a few more months, I might have added a lot of stuff that would have screwed it up. But in the end, I just wanted to get the thing out."[2]

DRAWBACKS

There were some drawbacks to Napster, however. One of them was that the Napster central servers weren't able to examine the real content of a file. Instead, they had to take for granted that the name of the file accurately represented what was really in the file. This meant that occasionally, a file claiming to be, for example, a Britney Spears song, could sometimes turn out to be a spoof—a different file entirely.

Critics of Napster also pointed out that it could have potentially dangerous complications. In essence, every time Napster users logged on, they opened up their computer's "front door" and invited other users in. By opening his or her hard drive up to other users, a Napster user was also theoretically becoming more vulnerable to hackers.

Another flaw was that although a user was able to see if someone was currently downloading something from his hard drive, it didn't always ensure that he would be polite and stay logged on to the system until the downloader was finished. If the user you were downloading from suddenly logged out of the system, your download would be abruptly cut off before you were able to copy the whole file.

But Napster's biggest drawback also ended up being the very thing that, in the end, contributed to its amazing popularity and growth. Although Napster dealt with MP3 files, which are relatively small in size, it moved a lot of those files back and forth—which ate up huge amounts of bandwidth. Bandwidth is like the highway that files travel on back and forth between a personal computer and the Internet. A person using Napster could download more than one file at a time and could also have more than one file being downloaded from him at the same time. This created a whole lot of incoming and outgoing traffic on the "bandwidth highway."

THE BANDWIDTH CRISIS

The first enthusiastic users of Napster were college students. This wasn't surprising—the program was founded by college students and passed from friend to friend by word of mouth. College students also tended to be the most avid music fans, and they had a lot of free time to spend searching for music. Most important, most college students were using a computer hooked up to their university's large computer system, which usually meant that they had really fast Internet connections and could download files very quickly.

The problem with students using the university systems, however, was that a centralized university computer system only had so much bandwidth available. Sure, they had far, far more bandwidth available than any individual computer owner alone. However, imagine all of the students in a major university suddenly hearing about and test-driving Napster at the same time. Every student, downloading and uploading simultaneously—it was a bandwidth nightmare, even for the huge university systems. This is how most of America first heard of Napster, from stories covering the "bandwidth crisis" on university campuses.

Shawn had finished a beta, or test, version of Napster by June 1, 1999, not long after he quit Northeastern. He distributed the beta to 30 friends, asking them to give him some feedback and advice; but there was one condition. He asked them to not pass the software on to anyone else. Of course, they did anyway. According to best accounts, the Napster software had been downloaded to 3,000 to 4,000 people within days of Shawn sending it out to his initial 30 friends. It spread like wildfire.

By the time that school was back in session for the 1999 fall semester, colleges suddenly realized that something was going on. From the beginning of the semester, university computer systems across the country were coming dangerously close to crashing. Something was eating all of their bandwidth. That something, of course, was Napster. Although Shawn hadn't spent a dime yet on publicity, Napster was already being distributed exponentially on a daily basis. And it was only a few months old.

Universities across the country scrambled to deal with the problem, with hundreds of schools quickly making the decision to ban Napster outright on their campuses. Oregon State University, one of the first to speak out against Napster in October 1999, reported that it was "in danger of going well over budget in bandwidth and had to act . . . [W]ith more students starting to use both Napster and download streaming video, there was a danger that bandwidth [use] would double every 90 days."[3]

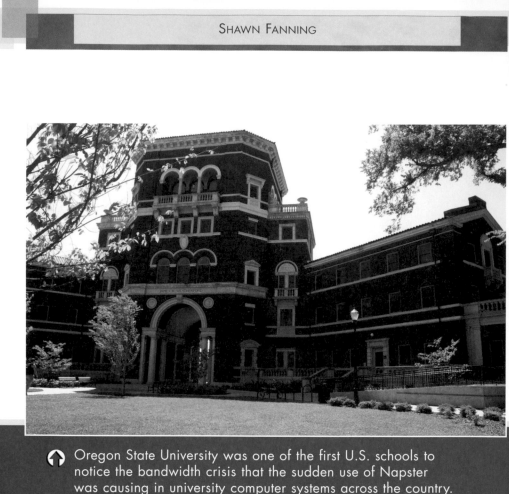

Oregon State University was one of the first U.S. schools to notice the bandwidth crisis that the sudden use of Napster was causing in university computer systems across the country. OSU made the decision in October 1999 to block access to Napster through its computer network, which was early in the fall semester.

Florida State University reported that Napster was eating up 20 to 30 percent of its bandwidth. The University of Illinois claimed a startling 75 to 80 percent. Hofstra and NYU both made the decision to block Napster from their school systems. And at all of the campuses that banned Napster, students protested in outrage.

A FLAW SECRETLY FIXED

One of the early flaws in the Napster program was a by-product of Napster's unexpected popularity. Napster quickly became so popular that the index of all of its users' files wouldn't fit on one central server. Shawn dealt with this problem by establishing more Napster central servers, each separate from the others. However, the drawback for Napster users was that every time they opened up Napster, they weren't really seeing the files for every single Napster user online at that moment; they were just seeing the files of the users who happened to also be routed to the same central server that they were on.

Savvy Napster users understood this, and it wasn't unusual for an experienced user to log on and scan the files indexed. If he didn't like what he saw, he could log out and log back in, hoping to be routed to a better index the second time.

By May 2000, the Napster team had finally found a way to fix the problem by linking all of the central servers together without the danger of the entire system crashing. Unfortunately, most Napster users never realized that the problem had been solved because Napster executives decided not to advertise the innovation. They feared that the news of the server link would be used against them somehow in the lawsuits that were pending against Napster.

NO BAD PUBLICITY?

However, some universities decided not to censor the computer activities of their students. Schools such as MIT and Harvard both saw the controversy as more of a right-to-privacy issue. Harvard released a statement that said, in part,

> We do not monitor or regulate users' choices of sites to visit, nor their activities at given sites. A selected ban on access to particular sites based on the content of those sites would be inconsistent with the values of broad inquiry and the exploration of ideas that Harvard, like other universities, has traditionally sought to protect.[4]

The battle lines were drawn, and suddenly every newspaper and magazine was reporting on this strange new computer program that was throwing university computer systems into chaos.

With each breaking news story on the controversy, more and more people across the country heard about Napster and the young genius who had created it, Shawn Fanning. As they went to check out the new site to see what the fuss was all about, it seemed as if the whole country was also marveling over Shawn, the nation's new pop culture icon.

CHAPTER FOUR

A VERY STRANGE YEAR

Before the fame set in, before the newspaper articles, and even before Shawn had finished writing the Napster program, John Fanning decided to have the idea incorporated into a company. In May 1999 Napster incorporated, providing it with many legal benefits and responsibilities. However, despite the formal incorporation, even at this early age Napster didn't operate like most other companies.

For one thing, the incorporation of Napster created a bit of controversy in and of itself. In a move that would later be portrayed in the media as ethically questionable, John made himself 70 percent owner of Napster, leaving only 30 percent ownership for Shawn. Apparently, this surprised Shawn when he learned of it. As a source reported to journalist Trevor Merriden, "I am told that this was done without Shawn Fanning's immediate knowledge or involvement. Newspapers have accurately reported the morally deplorable distribution of equity."[1]

Shawn has always declined to discuss his feelings about this early event, refusing to criticize his uncle's actions in the press. Despite whatever opinion he may have held about the split, publicly, Shawn seemed to shrug it off. After all, Napster wasn't really running like a formal company at the time, and there was no real money involved yet. Seventy percent of nothing is still nothing.

MAKING NAPSTER A REAL BUSINESS

This brings up another odd aspect of Napster. The goal for most companies is to turn a profit, and one of the first things that a fledgling company usually does to ensure it will turn a profit is devise a business plan, outlining how it will make money. Although Shawn knew that his program was going to be revolutionary (possibly even changing the way that other businesses operated online), in the beginning he never really tried to figure out how to make his program turn a profit on its own.

But that wasn't too surprising. Things like business plans are traditionally the responsibility of the company management—in this case, Shawn's more business-savvy uncle. Unfortunately, John didn't have a plan either. However, although he had no business plan, he instinctively knew that with something this big, there was bound to be potential for profit. John wanted to be sure that he was there when money was finally made.

There's a saying in the business world: "It takes money to make money." Napster certainly didn't have any money, but if they were going to be a real business they had to find a way to pay rent for office space, and to pay for office staff. As company manager, John Fanning set out to find investors to help finance the young company.

One of the first people John approached was his friend Yosi Amram. Amram, who had an

MBA from Harvard, agreed to invest in Napster. He also suggested another potential investor, tech entrepreneur Bill Bales. By the end of the summer of 1999, John Fanning had collected enough investment money from Amram and Bales to keep Napster running for at least the next six months. In addition, Bales became Napster's vice president of business development.

After Shawn unleashed the Napster program on the world in June 1999, it quickly became apparent that the group was onto something big. As the company watched the program spread across college campuses throughout the country, they knew that a tiger had just been let out of its cage. Napster was incorporated, the program was being distributed, and the company had investment money. Now it was time for them to start acting like a real business. They needed a real office. They needed a staff of programmers to deal with the problems and bugs that were certain to arise. They needed more financial backing. Most of all, they needed a CEO.

By September 1999, the decision was made to move the company to the West Coast. At the time, California was the hub of the computer world. Silicon Valley had become synonymous with the industry, and it was renowned as being not only the home of the programmers, but also the home of major investors. The group—John, Shawn, and two of Shawn's most trusted fellow programmers, Jordan Ritter and Sean Parker—boarded a plane for California.

Intoxicating Madness

Working out of a hotel for a few months (during which time Shawn and his friends gained a reputation for their frequent attempts to try to sneak into San Francisco–area bars), office space was finally found for Napster. The space that Napster rented in San Mateo, about twenty minutes south of San Francisco, was not the sort of place that most people would have imagined as being the office of a major media corporation. It consisted of a few empty rooms above a bank in a strip mall. But that didn't matter. The group needed the space to write code and plan strategy, not to throw parties.

With the office space secured, Shawn and his two new coprogrammers set about on the adventure of improving the Napster code. The atmosphere in the office was very reminiscent of the environment that Shawn had created for

himself when he was working on the beta version
of Napster, except now he had more company.
As Jordan Ritter was to reminisce later,

> In the beginning we were all driven by
> a kind of madness. Yes, I think that's
> the best description. I for one was

By the beginning of 2001, Napster had moved from its original
offices in San Mateo, California, to this storefront office building
in Redwood City, approximately ten miles (sixteen kilometers)
south of San Mateo. Both cities were part of the Silicon Valley
boom of the 1990s, as computer-related businesses sprang up
throughout the San Francisco Bay area.

simply overcome by the intoxicating madness of the thrill of the ride. I was pumping out code alongside the others, breaking for 30 minutes sometimes to have a white board discussion [with] whichever one of us would get stuck, and then heading back to our desks, headphones up, feet on the table, key-board in the lap, coding.[2]

Occasionally all of this focused work would be interrupted by the sudden achievement of an important goal, and a spontaneous party would break out in the office. At moments like this, Ritter adds, Shawn would "play some old school Notorious B.I.G., Snoop Dogg, or Dr. Dre and we'd all just start freaking out and doing some wacky [stuff]. Those were some fun times."[3]

While the nonstop coding frenzy took place in the office, John traveled around the area attempting to court more investment money for the venture and busied himself with the business side of the company. It was during this time that Bill Bales suggested someone for the CEO position. Eileen Richardson was a venture capitalist from the East Coast who initially seemed to fit in very well with the Napster environment. She was young and open-minded, and immediately understood what Shawn wanted to accomplish with Napster.

However, from a business perspective, many would later say that she was out of her league with Napster. Not only was this her first experience as a CEO, but her aggressive personality would later be called into question by analysts of Napster's early years. "In hindsight, Napster paid a price for hiring and sticking with a CEO who was confrontational and inexperienced for the Herculean task at hand," *BusinessWeek* magazine would later conclude.[4]

WALKING A FINE LINE

Unfortunately, negotiation, not confrontation, was what Napster was soon sorely in need of. Even before John Fanning incorporated Napster, he knew that the program was walking a fine line, legally. MP3 files had already come under fire from the major record labels, who had been protesting in the courts that ripping a song from a CD and transferring it to MP3 format was a violation of copyright law. Some manufacturers of portable MP3 players had already been sued. It seemed obvious that a company that enabled people to exchange MP3 files more easily was sure to catch the eye of the music industry as well.

Early in Napster's history, John had contacted Seth Greenstein, an expert in copyright law, and asked for his advice. Greenstein was encouraging. He pointed out that in theory, Napster was simply exchanging files between two people, and the files themselves were not marked as being copyrighted material. In other words, Napster

As the Napster craze caught on across the nation, the Napster interface screen was soon seen on computer monitors in computer labs and dorm rooms everywhere. Most users weren't concerned about the legality of the program, assuming that if it were illegal it wouldn't be so popular and widespread. However, although most people didn't suspect that it was illegal, most people did consider it too good to be true.

was technically just the middleman, not the criminal. In Greenstein's argument, all of the criminal activity was being done by the Napster users, not by Napster itself. This opinion comforted John, giving him the courage to continue on with the formation of the company. However, Greenstein's parting advice was more ominous. He warned John to expect a fight. By his estimation, Napster had about a 98 percent chance of being sued eventually.[5]

That eventuality came about much faster than anyone expected it to. Because Napster was spreading like wildfire on college campuses and prompting massive amounts of media attention, it caught the eye of the record companies almost immediately. By the time that Richardson became the company's CEO in September 1999 (less than three months after the program was released), calls were coming into Napster's new offices. The major recording companies, fronted by the Recording Industry Association of America (RIAA), were calling. And they were angry.

A New David to the RIAA Goliath

Shawn should have been flattered by the attention. He was now a part of a long tradition of media innovators who had been threatened by the prospect of a copyright infringement lawsuit by the recording establishment.

In the 1920s, the recording establishment had challenged the radio industry, claiming that no one would willingly buy music records if they could hear the same music on the radio for free. The radio broadcasting industry won the battle, and before long, it became obvious that radio actually boosted, rather than diminished, record sales.

In the 1970s, the invention of audiocassette tapes caused mass panic in the music industry, with the RIAA claiming that the availability of cassettes was encouraging people to make bootleg tapes of copyrighted material. Similarly, in the early 1980s, manufacturers of the VCR were sued by film and television studios, which claimed that videocassette recording was also in violation of copyright law.

In both instances, the courts ruled that the recording technology did not violate copyright law. Furthermore, neither one of the technologies were ever proven to have hurt sales of prerecorded material (in fact, videocassettes ended up generating a great deal of money for the film and television studios).

THE RECORD SALES ARGUMENT

One of the recurring complaints that the RIAA leveled against Napster was that the practice of downloading music would lead to decreased CD sales and decreased profit for the record companies. However, Napster fans consistently argued against this assumption, saying that on the contrary, Napster encouraged record sales.

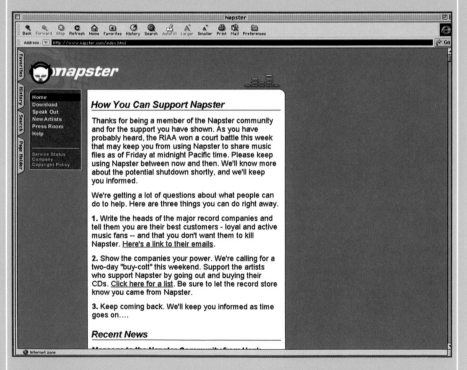

The Napster.com home page announcement as of July 28, 2000, instructed users about how they could help support Napster if the site was shut down for legal reasons.

The pro-Napster view held that if people discovered an interesting band through Napster online, they would actually be more inclined to go out and buy the band's CDs, especially since people were likely to want the features that weren't available to them from the download, such as liner notes and lyrics.

If one was to look exclusively at record sales to prove or disprove this argument, it seems that the Napster supporters might have had a point. Contrary to the RIAA's theory, record sales in both 1999 and 2000 actually increased. However, in 2001, the year that Napster was shut down, worldwide sales of CDs fell 5 percent.

By 1992, it seemed as though cases such as these had been definitively settled with the Audio Home Recording Act. This act made it entirely legal for people to make a recording of copyrighted material for their own personal use. To take things a step further, the act even ruled that a person could give a copy of the recorded material to a friend. The law only prohibited someone from distributing or selling mass copies of a homemade recording.

As Napster viewed the case, it was operating under the guidelines set by the Audio Home Recording Act. Napster made no profit. Napster itself wasn't even doing the copying; its users were. And there were no mass copies being made, technically—each user was making his own individual copies. The fact that several millions of users combined together might be considered "mass copying" was swept quickly under the carpet by the Napster team. On the whole, Napster was fairly confident.

Many legal experts also seemed to be optimistic that Napster had a good chance of winning a key victory. Public opinion was certainly in favor of Napster. The timing was good. In the late 1990s, a series of musical recording artists (most notably Prince) had publicly criticized recording companies, complaining to the music media that the companies were getting rich at the expense of the artists.

Music fans were also making a recurring complaint that most CDs that were released only had one or two good songs on them, the rest being filler. In general, people were not in the mood to be sympathetic toward the record companies. Napster's arrival seemed like the comeuppance that the record companies deserved. Napster looked like a courageous little David, hurling rocks at a huge, evil RIAA

While Napster was being accused of "mass copying" and piracy, illegally duplicated CDs were flooding the United States from various foreign countries. This material was in violation of all international copyright laws. Although the CDs were destroyed when found (as with this pile of illegal CDs discovered in China), a majority of the illegal material was never intercepted by the authorities.

Goliath—and having likeable, photogenic Shawn Fanning as the Napster poster boy didn't hurt Napster's case any, either.

The recording companies sensed that they weren't guaranteed a victory against Napster in the courts. They also realized that public sentiment was against them. Although they were threatening lawsuits, at first it seemed as though they were more likely to open negotiations with Napster to reach a settlement.

Logically, most people expected Napster to agree to a settlement that would give the record companies a stake in the Napster business in exchange for the rights to reproduce the copyrighted songs being traded on the Internet. At the very worst, people feared that the deal would force Napster to start charging a small user fee in order to pay royalties for the copyrighted material. But few people really expected the case to go all the way to court.

THE BALL DROPS

However, the negotiations did not go well. Hilary Rosen, the president of the RIAA, represented the record companies during the talks. As the new CEO, Eileen Richardson represented Napster. From the beginning, people involved in the negotiations described them as being "a clash of cultures and monster egos."[6] Although the RIAA might have been initially interested in reaching a settlement, Richardson was reportedly generally inflexible in her insistence that Napster was legally and morally in the right.

Hilary Rosen, the then president of the Recording Industry Association of America (RIAA), testifies during a hearing about online entertainment in 2001, as Gerry Kearby of Liquid Audio looks on. Many people speculated later that it was Rosen's personality conflict with Eileen Richardson, the CEO of Napster, that fueled tension between the two companies and created a more hostile legal situation.

Further, Richardson's abrasive style came to be a problem. *Business Week* summarized the communication breakdown:

> One Napster employee, who declined to be identified, heard Richardson yelling on the phone at Frank Creighton, the head of RIAA's antipiracy group. Richardson also had face-to-face meetings with Hilary B. Rosen . . . that did not go well, according to people familiar with the discussions.[7]

Before long, the RIAA was no longer interested in continuing negotiations with Napster. In their view, Richardson had made it clear that Napster was not willing to make any deal with the record companies.

It all seemed crazy. Napster was the most widely downloaded application on the Internet, with users growing in record numbers every day. Despite this fact, it hadn't earned a penny of profit as a business. Shawn Fanning was one of the country's most popular personalities, but he had almost no control over the business aspect of

HOW MANY PEOPLE USED NAPSTER?

Pinning down the exact number of Napster users in the history of the company is difficult. Because Napster utilized a central server system, we can get a decent estimate, but it doesn't take into account some of the things that wouldn't be recorded by the server, such as users logging on under more than one screen name, or users logging on through someone else's computer.

At the height of Napster's legal battles (when it was getting maximum media coverage), an online tracking service estimated that in the six months between February and July 2000, the number of users grew from just over 1 million to 6.7 million. The same service estimated that the program was running on 10 percent of American computers. A conservative estimate suggests that the total number of Americans who downloaded music using Napster was about 58 million. As impressive as this number is, it doesn't take into account the users in Canada or overseas. The worldwide total of Napster users would be far higher. Unfortunately, statistics were never gathered on the overseas implications of Napster.

the program that he had created. And at Napster, everything was about to get even crazier.

The ball dropped in December 1999, when the RIAA and eighteen record companies joined together to formally file a lawsuit against

Napster. As *Business Week* concluded afterward, "When it came time to compromise, Napster waited too long to bring in seasoned minds that could have salvaged a deal with the record labels . . . It left the record industries with no choice but to gain control or shut them down."[8]

The year had started with Shawn dropping out of college to work on his program. Four months later, he had minority ownership in his own company. A month after that, he released his program and it quickly became one of the most downloaded programs in the country. Two months later, record companies were threatening to sue him. And by the end of 1999, they had. It had been a really weird year for Shawn Fanning. Unfortunately, the year 2000 was about to be even worse.

CHAPTER FIVE

THE NAPSTER BATTLE

B y this time, Shawn was now famous. He was commonly known as the genius kid who was scaring the pants off of a multibillion-dollar-a-year industry. Despite the fact that Shawn seemed to be everywhere, he was not a media hound. He never actively courted the press. After all, fame wasn't what inspired Shawn to write the program in the first place. As he admitted in an interview at the time:

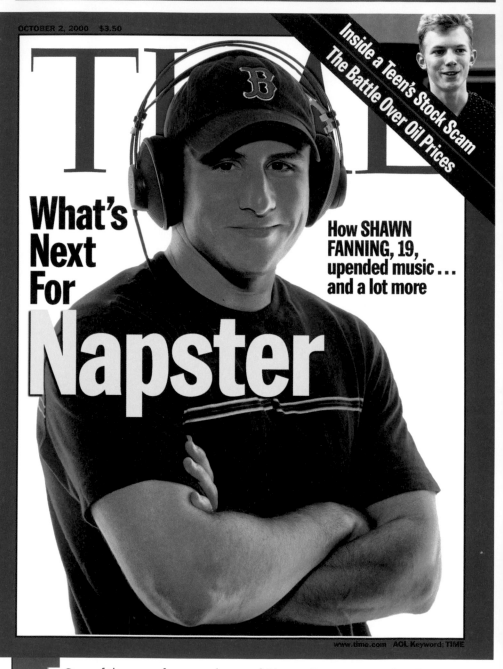

OCTOBER 2, 2000 $3.50

TIME

What's Next For
Napster

Inside a Teen's Stock Scam
The Battle Over Oil Prices

How SHAWN FANNING, 19, upended music ... and a lot more

www.time.com   AOL Keyword: TIME

One of the most famous photos of Shawn Fanning was this *Time* magazine cover for the week of October 2, 2000. Although media interest in Shawn grew quickly, he seemed confused and surprised by the attention. He never considered himself to be in the same league as the musicians he idolized, so he couldn't understand why he should be on the cover of major magazines.

I'm naturally shy, so I hate standing out in a group of people. It's still a little bit strange being in the public eye. People even recognize me in the gym—it's kind of hard to get a solid workout. It was the last thing I ever expected when I was writing the software at Northeastern. If you're a musician or an artist, and you're working hard to succeed, you know that fame is part of that, but not when you're writing software.[1]

Part of what made Shawn uncomfortable was that he still saw himself as just another fan, rather than as a star. After all, being a fan was one of the things that motivated him to write the Napster program. He loved music, and there were certain bands that he especially loved; bands that he respected and idolized. But that was about to change.

ENTER METALLICA

One of Shawn's favorite bands in high school had been Metallica. In fact, he even briefly played guitar in a band that covered Metallica tunes. That's what made an announcement in

April 2000 even more heartbreaking for Shawn. By then, he had come to terms with the fact that the record companies were suing his company. He had gotten over being really worried about it; he trusted in the Napster lawyers who were optimistic that the suit would come out in Napster's favor. Besides, a lawsuit filed by a huge industry didn't seem that personal. It was just business.

But the next lawsuit was entirely different. On April 13, 2000, Metallica filed a lawsuit against Napster. They claimed that Napster had violated not only copyright laws, but also the Racketeer Influenced and Corrupt Organizations Act (RICO). The RICO act was typically used to prosecute Mafia members for illegal organized-crime activities. Shortly afterward, rap artist Dr. Dre filed a similar suit.

Shawn was stunned. He had created the Napster program because of his love for music, and now it seemed as if one of his favorite bands was trying to destroy him. And Metallica and Dr. Dre were not alone. The RIAA began a campaign to encourage many of its recording artists to publicly speak out against Napster, hoping to turn the tide of public opinion away from the popular program.

Things didn't quite work the way that the RIAA planned, however. More artists were indeed coming out publicly against Napster, but unexpectedly, some, such as Dave Matthews and Moby, were also coming out in support of the program. In addition, there was some backlash against the artists that condemned Napster. Metallica fans

A tense moment occurred during the Senate Judiciary Committee hearings in July 2000, when Roger McGuinn *(seated left)*, a member of the 1960s band the Byrds, and Lars Ulrich *(leaning in, center)*, the drummer of Metallica, angrily confronted Napster's new CEO, Hank Barry *(seated right)*. Many musicians publicly took sides both for and against Napster during the controversy.

across the United States turned on the band. Hackers began to break into Metallica Web sites, posting pro-Napster messages. Some people vowed to sell all of their Metallica albums in protest.

Even Metallica members themselves may have had some second thoughts, according to journalist Joseph Menn. On May 3, 2000, Metallica decided to host a media event to underscore their anger at Napster. Metallica drummer Lars Ulrich arrived at the Napster office in San Mateo to publicly deliver a list of over 300,000 Napster users who had down-loaded Metallica songs—a list Metallica was able to compile after reviewing the records of Napster's central server activity. However, in his book *All the Rave*, Menn relates that the meeting didn't turn out quite as Ulrich planned:

> The new generation gap got its loudest display when Ulrich spoke from the podium. Protesters shouted at him to shut up and called him a sellout . . . Showing up with a lawyer was about the least "rock star" move that Ulrich could make, and from the moment he realized that Napster was housed in the decrepit building over a bank, he grew more and

more uncomfortable . . . When the doors opened at Napster's fourth-floor office, the employees came up to him and told them what fans they were and how they had gone to Metallica concerts in junior high. Ulrich seemed to slump. "I really don't want to sue you," he

The T-shirt read around the world: Shawn Fanning's famous fashion statement at the 2000 MTV Video Music Awards won Napster new fans and sympathy across the globe. Shawn (with fellow presenter Carson Daly) chose to wear the T-shirt of his favorite band, Metallica, in spite of the fact that Metallica had come out loudly against Napster in the media.

said. "All I want is for artists who want to get paid to get paid."[2]

Despite the negative backlash from Metallica fans, the publicity stunt had the desired effect with Napster. In a decision that dismayed Napster supporters, the company caved in to Metallica's request, and on May 10, they blocked from the system the 317,377 users that Metallica had identified as having downloaded the band's music.

Despite what his company executives might have decided to do, Shawn refused to let Metallica get the last word. Shawn's newfound fame allowed him a few opportunities to work the media as well, and in September 2000 Shawn was invited to be a presenter at the MTV Video Music Awards. To the shock of everyone and the complete admiration of all of his fans, Shawn walked onto the stage at the awards show wearing a Metallica T-shirt. The television cameras quickly panned the audience until they found and focused on Lars Ulrich, who glared at the young celebrity. Shawn never flinched; he just grinned slyly at the cameras. For Napster supporters, it was a glorious moment—one that gained Shawn and his company additional sympathy and respect.

LINES ARE DRAWN IN THE MUSIC COMMUNITY

Although Napster seemed like a great thing to most average citizens, music artists tended to see the issue from a completely different perspective. After all, they were the ones who were trying to make a living from the music that was being traded for free. Even so, musicians were far from being in total agreement about Napster. While musicians including Metallica, Dr. Dre, Eminem, Peter Gabriel, and Sheryl Crow spoke out against Napster, there were a surprising number of artists who saw Napster as a positive thing for the music industry as well as for the fans. Neil Young, the Grateful Dead, Moby, Courtney Love, Prince, and Dave Matthews all spoke out in favor of Napster. Chuck D of Public Enemy was one of Napster's most enthusiastic supporters, telling *Newsweek* in a June 2000 article, "I'm down for a parallel business even if it is parasitic. Napster is the new radio. It's the most exciting thing since rap, disco and the Beatles."

CALM BEFORE THE STORM

In May 2000, Napster had another brief stroke of good fortune. An investment company named Hummer Winblad stepped forward following some negotiations and offered to invest $15 million in Napster. This was money that was sorely needed to fund the legal battle still on the horizon.

Fortunately for Napster, the windfall came with an added bonus: a new CEO. One of Hummer Winblad's managing partners, Hank Barry, stepped in, replacing Eileen Richardson as the head of Napster. Almost immediately, Barry hired David Boies, a famous antitrust lawyer who had a substantial background in copyright law.

Napster itself was also still growing in users, profiting as much from the negative media coverage as it had from the positive. It seemed like every time Napster was mentioned in the media—for any reason—new users immediately logged on. Napster wasn't solely the domain of college students anymore, either. As Shawn said in an interview at the time, "It's been adopted by people of all ages. My parents are into it too, which is really strange for me . . . I just got an email from a ninety-one-year-old [user]."[3]

Napster was beginning to try to find a solution to its income problems as well; or at least a temporary one. Early on in the business, Shawn and Sean Parker had worked together with a graphic designer named Sam Hanks to design a company logo for Napster. The result—a slightly anime-styled cat wearing headphones—had become a pop culture touchstone. Everyone recognized it. Napster began licensing the logo on

T-shirts, and it proved to be a successful move. For a moment, things were beginning to look up for Napster.

All things considered, life wasn't going too badly for Shawn, either. He tried to stay focused on everyday things, such as programming and working out. His day-to-day life hadn't changed much, which was surprising considering the tangle of events that had been unfolding around him. He had rented an apartment just a few minutes away from the Napster office in San Mateo, and Sean Parker chipped in as his roommate.

He still worked out daily at 24 Hour Fitness and played pick-up basketball games whenever he got a chance. Residents of San Mateo reported seeing him around town often, always dressed down in his now-trademark T-shirt, baseball cap, and jeans. Anyone who didn't know any better would never suspect that he was part of a company that had just received $15 million in financial backing, much less that this average-looking kid had thought up the whole idea of Napster in the first place. There weren't too many people left who didn't know any better, though. Shawn was on the cover of various magazines on the newsstands. Everyone knew him.

As far as splurges or indulgences went, however, Shawn didn't see the point. Shawn's one big splurge was his new dream car: a tricked-out Mazda RX-7, complete with a customized sound system, of course. Although most people assumed that Shawn's position in Napster meant that he had become very wealthy very quickly, this wasn't the case. Shawn was a salaried employee at the company. He was doing well, but not extraordinarily well. There was one thing about his salary that did impress him, however. "I have been able to get my parents out of debt," he told *People* magazine. "That is cool."[4]

A VERDICT AND APPEAL

Unfortunately, this brief period in 2000 was just the calm before the storm for both Shawn and Napster. The lawsuit that the RIAA had filed against Napster at the end of 1999 was still pending, and everyone was waiting to go to court. Along with monetary damages, the suit had also contained a request for an injunction against Napster that would require the site to be shut down permanently. Finally, word came in to the Napster offices that the case was about to be decided.

On the morning of July 26, 2000, Shawn and his team of Napster lawyers entered a San

Francisco courtroom to face the verdict. John Fanning did not attend, explaining that he expected that the decision—whichever way it went—would be appealed, and the case would truly be decided in an appellate court.

The decision was made by U.S. District Judge Marilyn Patel, and after two hours of argument, the judge ruled against Napster. The injunction was granted, and Napster was informed that it had two days to shut down operations online. Tears welled up in Shawn's eyes, and his legal team struggled to cobble together a press release on the verdict. They had been so sure that the hearing would be ruled in their favor that they hadn't even bothered to prepare a statement beforehand.

When the news of the decision broke, Napster users went into a frenzy, trying to download as much as possible before Napster went offline. It was estimated that at least 600,000 users logged on per day during the next two days. However, the panic proved to be premature. On July 28, just nine hours before it was supposed to shut down, Napster won a stay of the injunction on appeal.

The appeals court decided that there had been "substantial questions" regarding Judge

Patel's injunction ruling, and it concluded that the injunction request needed to be reheard. Napster was legally allowed to operate until a ruling came in on the second injunction hearing. That hearing happened in October 2000, and at the conclusion of it, Napster and the RIAA were advised that the final injunction ruling would be announced in November.

GOOD OMENS

While Shawn waited on the ruling, he had plenty to keep him busy. The publicity over the Napster controversy had caught the attention of the U.S. government, and Shawn was called in to testify before the United States Senate Committee on the Judiciary. At that time, the committee had the reputation for being very politically conservative, and everyone expected them to come down hard on Shawn.

However, on October 9, when Shawn testified before the committee, he made a favorable impression on the panel. Committee members seemed sympathetic to Shawn in interviews that they gave afterwards. Even the committee's most conservative member, chairman Orrin Hatch of Utah, seemed won over by Shawn by the end of the testimony. It seemed like a good sign for Napster.

On Halloween 2000, Napster received what seemed like another good omen. German media giant Bertelsmann announced that it had made a deal with Napster to go into business together. It appeared to be a stunning coup for Napster. Bertelsmann owned BMG, one of the largest record companies in the world—and one of the companies that had been named in the RIAA suit against Napster. The terms of the agreement were that Bertelsmann would withdraw from the RIAA lawsuit and allow Napster to trade its inventory of copyrighted songs on the Internet. In return, Napster would begin charging a subscription fee to users in order to pay for royalties, and Bertelsmann would be given a major share of Napster.

However, despite this deal, there was still a lawsuit pending. Napster didn't forget that there was still a chance that they would win the lawsuit that the RIAA had filed against them and be declared innocent of copyright violation entirely. If that happened, they wouldn't need to charge users a subscription fee because they wouldn't have to pay royalties for any of the songs traded with their program. Napster had an "escape plan" written into the Bertelsmann deal just in case that happened. If Napster won the upcoming suit, then the

WHY THE JUDICIARY COMMITTEE?

When Napster made downloading MP3 files so popular in such a short amount of time, the RIAA was not the only organization to take notice. Political leaders across the United States also became concerned about how the practice might change the way that business in general was conducted. Congress was then called to conduct an independent investigation on the practice of downloading and trading MP3 files. The investigation was held in the form of a U.S. Senate Judiciary Committee, who called upon Shawn to testify in October 2000.

The Judiciary Committee investigation was entirely independent of the court case that Napster was involved in at the time, and the committee's decisions had no direct bearing on the outcome of Shawn's case. However, the Judiciary Committee did have the ability to advise that new laws be passed on the basis of the testimony they heard—laws that could possibly benefit Napster, despite what the ruling was in the Napster court case. Although the Judiciary Committee was publicly very sympathetic with Shawn, they ultimately decided not to create any new laws based on his testimony, and the investigation didn't legally help Napster in any way.

terms of the Bertlesmann deal would be open to renegotiation. Napster, despite the appearance of trying to hedge its bets with a last-minute deal, was still hanging on to a little hope.

THE DEATH KNELL

The wait for the final decision took longer than expected, but when it finally came, it was a death knell. On February 12, 2001, the Ninth Circuit Court of Appeals finally handed down its verdict.

Shawn Fanning "dressed to impress" during the Senate Judiciary Committee hearings in Washington, D.C., in 2000. Many senators, such as Democratic senator Dianne Feinstein of California *(left)*, reported later that they were impressed with Shawn's testimony and sympathized with Napster in general. Unfortunately, the committee decided not to intervene legally in favor of Napster.

The unanimous ruling of the panel was that Napster had been operating in violation of music copyrights. Napster requested an appeal, but in June 2001 the request was denied. Napster was ordered to immediately prevent any copyrighted material from being traded via their program.

However, the deal with Bertelsmann now went into effect, and because of it, Napster was still able to allow users to trade BMG copyrighted songs. Even so, the limitations on the program were severe, and Napster was just not the same anymore. Napster had hoped that other record companies would be interested in making a deal with them similar to the one that Bertelsmann had made, but unfortunately, that was not to be. Napster had waited too long to negotiate, and in the meantime, most of the other record companies had developed their own Napster-like sites where downloads of their company's copyrighted material could be made for a subscription fee.

There was also some last-minute hope that perhaps the government—which had seemed sympathetic toward Napster during the United States Judiciary Committee hearings—might step in and pass a new law that would void the court ruling and favor Napster. Unfortunately, that didn't pan out either. On July 1, 2001, Napster, as the world had known it, was dismantled forever.

SHAWN FANNING—DESPITE EVERYTHING

On June 3, 2002, beset by legal debt and unable to find sufficient financial assistance from any investing company, Napster filed for Chapter 11 bankruptcy. It had acquired $101 million in liability, not even counting what it owed in the legal settlements to the record companies. Eventually, Roxio, the maker of Toast CD-burning software, bought the rights to the Napster name and iconography in a bankruptcy auction. Napster returned to the Internet as a subscription-based music downloading program. But by that time, Shawn, John, and all of the rest of the original Napster team had left.

In almost exactly two years' time, Shawn Fanning's obsessive idea had rocketed from the obscurity of being a test download distributed to thirty people, to the heights of being the most popular computer program in the country, and then back down to the depths of obscurity once more. It had been a crazy, emotionally wrenching experience for everyone involved, especially Shawn.

Despite everything that Shawn had been through with Napster, all evidence shows that he came out of it much the same as he went in. He reflected positively on the experience later, saying,

> I started out with the intention of learning about Windows programming and trying to solve an interesting problem. [Napster] certainly far exceeded

Long after Shawn Fanning's association with the company he founded was over, the Napster logo was still in the public eye when the new owners of the company name began licensing "Napster" products for sale in stores. Here, Napster gift cards and MP3 players are displayed on the shelves at a Best Buy in East Palo Alto, California, in 2005.

my expectations. I didn't walk away
with a ton of money, but I earned a
salary while I was working obviously
and I was able to make a little bit of
money in the process. If I had just
cashed out [in the beginning], it's possible I could have just blown it all.[5]

Success hadn't changed this good-natured,
shy kid from blue-collar Harwich, and fortunately, neither had failure. All of those adjectives
that people had been using for him at the height
of his fame still seemed to apply. He was a
gearhead—and a renegade. He was a wunderkind,
but still average in many respects. He was sweet,
driven, unassuming—despite everything he'd
been up against. But maybe it was Shawn's biological father, Joe Rando, who finally summed
it all up best. "I'm completely impressed with
Shawn, but not because of the public reasons—
because of the person he is," Rando said. "It
didn't go to his head, which is pretty amazing."[6]

TIMELINE

November 1980—	Shawn Fanning is born in Rockland, Massachusetts.
1995—	A German company, Fraunhofer Gesellschaft, applies for a patent for the MP3 technology in the United States.
1996—	Fanning receives his first computer, an Apple Macintosh 512+.
September 1998—	Fanning enrolls in Northeastern University in Boston, Massachusetts.
January 1999—	Fanning drops out of Northeastern University.
May 1999—	Napster is incorporated.
June 1999—	Fanning sends a test version of Napster to thirty friends.
September 1999—	Napster moves its offices to San Mateo, California.
	Eileen Richardson becomes Napster's first CEO.
October 1999—	Universities across the country begin banning Napster.
December 1999—	Napster is sued by the RIAA and eighteen record companies.

TIMELINE

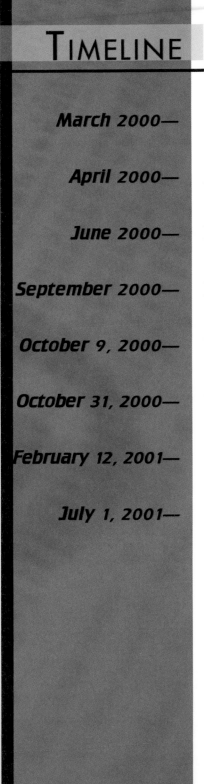

March 2000— Gnutella, Napster's first serious competitor, is released.

April 2000— Metallica files a lawsuit against Napster.

June 2000— Napster is ordered to cease operating but wins a stay on appeal.

September 2000— Fanning wears a Metallica T-shirt to the MTV Video Music Awards.

October 9, 2000— Fanning testifies before the U.S. Judiciary Committee.

October 31, 2000— Napster announces a partnership with Bertlesmann.

February 12, 2001— The Ninth Circuit Court of Appeals rules against Napster.

July 1, 2001— Napster goes off-line.

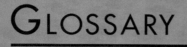

GLOSSARY

antitrust Referring to laws that protect trade and commerce against unfair trade practices and monopolies.

appropriate To set apart and make use of if necessary.

bandwidth The amount of data that can be sent over a network connection in a specific period of time. It is usually expressed in bits per second (bps), kilobits per second (kbps), or megabits per second (mps).

Chapter 11 bankruptcy A reorganization of debt when a troubled business is unable to pay its debtors or contractors.

copyright The legal protection given to authors and artists of original published literary, musical, or artistic works to prevent unauthorized copying of their work.

injunction A court order issued to a person or party that prohibits them from continuing or engaging in a certain activity.

Internet Relay Chat (IRC) A live, multiuse chat network that operates over the Internet. Users log on to a channel and can join a text conference in real time.

Microsoft Windows One of the first user-friendly operating systems, introduced in 1985 by Microsoft. It consists of a graphical environment that simplifies disk operating system (DOS) commands and programs. Users can run programs by using a mouse to click on commands, graphical icons, and folders.

peer-to-peer (P2P) Referring to a file-sharing network where users who are logged on can download files from other users who are logged on at the same time.

ripping Copying or burning audio or visual data from one media form, such as CDs or DVDs, to a hard drive.

robot Also known as a spider, a software program that search engines use to surf the World Wide Web.

stay A judicial order that forbids or stops an action until a specific event occurs or the order is lifted.

streaming video A series of moving images sent over the Internet in a compressed form and displayed for the viewer as they arrive.

Unix A computer operating system developed by AT&T and Bell Labs in 1969 that allowed for multiple users and multitasking. Unix was used to develop the Internet.

FOR MORE INFORMATION

American Computer Museum
2304 North 7th Avenue, Suite B
Bozeman, MT 59715
(406) 582-1288
Web site: http://www.compustory.com

Computer History Museum
1401 N. Shoreline Boulevard
Mountain View, CA 94043
(650) 810-1010
Web site: http://www.computerhistory.org

WEB SITES

Due to the changing nature of Internet links, the
Rosen Publishing Group, Inc., has developed an
online list of Web sites related to the subject of this
book. This site is updated regularly. Please use this
link to access the list:

http://www.rosenlinks.com/icb/shfa

Alderman, John. *Sonic Boom: Napster, MP3 and the New Pioneers of Music.* Cambridge, England: Perseus Publishing, 2001.

Ante, Spencer, Stephen Brull, Dennis Berman, and Mike France. "Inside Napster." *Business Week,* August 14, 2000, pp. 112–120.

Greenfield, Karl Taro. "Meet the Napster." *Time,* October 2, 2000.

Menn, Joseph. *All the Rave.* New York, NY: Crown Business, 2003.

Merriden, Trevor. *Irresistible Forces.* Oxford, England: Capstone Publishing, 2001.

Mitten, Christopher. *Shawn Fanning.* Brookfield, CT: Twenty-First Century Books, 2002.

Thompson, Clifford, ed. "Shawn Fanning." *Current Biography Yearbook 2000.* New York, NY: H. W. Wilson Company, 2000.

BIBLIOGRAPHY

Alderman, John. *Sonic Boom: Napster, MP3 and the New Pioneers of Music.* Cambridge, England: Perseus Publishing, 2001.

Ante, Spencer. "Shawn Fanning's Struggle." *BusinessWeek.* May 1, 2000, pp. 197–198.

Ante, Spencer, Stephen Brull, Dennis Berman, and Mike France. "Inside Napster." *BusinessWeek,* August 14, 2000, pp. 112–120.

Brown, Janelle. "MP3 Free-For-All." Salon.com. February 3, 2003. Retrieved September 10, 2005 (http://archive.salon.com/ tech/feature/ 200/02/03/napster/index.html).

Cohen, Warren. "Napster Is Rocking the Music Industry." *U.S. News and World Report,* March 6, 2000, p. 41.

Greenfield, Karl Taro. "Meet the Napster." *Time,* October 2, 2000.

Heilemann, John. "Shawn Fanning's New Tune." *Business,* May 2005, pp. 38–41.

Kover, Amy. "Who's Afraid of This Kid?" *Fortune,* March 20, 2000, pp. 129–131.

Levy, Steven, Brad Stone, N'Gai Croal, Jennifer Tanaka, Arian Campo-Flores, Jamie Reno, Andrew Murr, and Pat Wingert. "The Noisy

War Over Napster." *Newsweek*, June 6, 2000, pp. 46–53.

Menn, Joseph. *All the Rave*. New York, NY: Crown Business, 2003.

Merriden, Trevor. *Irresistible Forces*. Oxford, England: Capstone Publishing, 2001.

Miller, Samantha. "Slipped Disc: Facing the Music in Court." *People Weekly*, August 14, 2000, pp. 73–74.

Mitten, Christopher. *Shawn Fanning*. Brookfield, CT: Twenty-First Century Books, 2002.

"Napster." Wikipedia: The Free Encyclopedia. Retrieved August 20, 2005 (http://en.wikipedia.org/wiki/Napster).

Sheffield, Rob. "The Most Dangerous Man in the Music Biz." *Rolling Stone*, June 7, 2000.

Sheffield, Rob. "People of the Year: Shawn Fanning." *Rolling Stone*, December 14, 2000, pp. 142–144.

Thompson, Clifford, ed. "Shawn Fanning." *Current Biography Yearbook 2000*. New York, NY: H. W. Wilson Company, 2000.

Wingfield, Nick. "Napster Boy—Interrupted." *Wall Street Journal*, Eastern Edition, October 1, 2002.

SOURCE NOTES

CHAPTER ONE

1. Spencer Ante, "Shawn Fanning's Struggle," *Business Week*, May 1, 2000, p. 197.

2. Joseph Menn, *All the Rave* (New York, NY: Crown Business, 2003), p. 14.

3. Ibid., p. 16.

4. Ibid., p. 15.

5. Karl Taro Greenfield, "Meet the Napster," *Time*, October 2, 2000.

6. Ante, p. 198.

7. Menn, p. 15.

8. Ibid., p. 17.

CHAPTER TWO

1. Janelle Brown, "MP3 Free-For-All," Salon.com, February 3, 2003. Retrieved September 10, 2005 (http://archive.salon.com/ tech/feature/ 200/02/03/napster/index.html).

2. Joseph Menn, *All the Rave* (New York, NY: Crown Business, 2003), p. 35.

3. Trevor Merriden, *Irresistible Forces* (Oxford, England: Capstone Publishing, 2001), p. 7.

4. Ibid., p. 7.

5. Menn, p. 52.

6. Menn, p. 52.

7. Menn, p. 53.

8. Menn, p. 54.

Chapter Three

1. Joseph Menn, *All the Rave* (New York, NY: Crown Business, 2003), p. 34.

2. Karl Taro Greenfield, "Meet the Napster," *Time*, October 2, 2000.

3. Trevor Merriden, *Irresistible Forces* (Oxford, England: Capstone Publishing, 2001), p. 16.

4. Ibid., p. 19.

Chapter Four

1. Trevor Merriden, *Irresistible Forces* (Oxford, England: Capstone Publishing, 2001), p. 9.

2. Ibid., p. 10.

3. Ibid., p. 11.

4. Spencer Ante, Stephen Brull, Dennis Berman, and Mike France, "Inside Napster," *Business Week*, August 14, 2000, p. 116.

5. Joseph Menn, *All the Rave* (New York, NY: Crown Business, 2003), p. 68.

6. Spencer, Brull, Berman, and France, p. 116.

7. Spencer, Brull, Berman, and France, p. 117.

8. Spencer, Brull, Berman, and France, p. 116

CHAPTER FIVE

1. Rob Sheffield, "People of the Year: Shawn Fanning," *Rolling Stone*, December 14, 2000, p. 142.

2. Joseph Menn, *All the Rave* (New York, NY: Crown Business, 2003), p. 145.

3. Sheffield, p. 142.

4. Samantha Miller, "Slipped Disc: Facing the Music in Court," *People Weekly*, August 14, 2000, p. 74.

5. Nick Wingfield, "Napster Boy—Interrupted," *Wall Street Journal*, Eastern Edition, October 1, 2002, p. B-1.

6. Menn, p. 322.

INDEX

About the Author

Renee Ambrosek is a writer—who also publishes under her married name, Renee Graves—and an avid and enthusiastic music fan. After researching Shawn Fanning's story, and coming to a better understanding of it and Napster, she was glad for the opportunity to share what she learned with a younger audience. Ms. Ambrosek lives in Memphis, Tennessee, with her husband, Alan, and her daughter, Gabriella.

Photo Credits

Designer: Nelson Sá
Editor: Leigh Ann Cobb
Photo Researcher: Jeffrey Wendt